The Very Best of Maya Angelou

The Voice of Inspiration

FRANK JOHNSON

ISBN: 1503274284
ISBN-13: 978-1503274280

DISCLAIMER

All quotes within this book are in the words of Maya Angelou. Although every effort has been taken to ensure the accuracy of all text, the author apologises in the event of any mistakes.

CONTENTS

INTRODUCTION

Although best known as a prolific poet and author, Maya Angelou was a woman of many talents, also including acting, dancing and singing. She was also renowned for her wisdom and her outspokenness on topics of social and racial equality.

Having been a notable activist in the Civil Rights movement in America, Angelou was very active on the lecture circuit, making several appearances a week, continuing well into her eighties. She has been a voice of inspiration for many around the world, known for her honesty, bluntness and courage.

Though sometimes criticised for her unorthodox style, Maya Angelou won many awards for her writing and unique recitals (the most notable of which possibly being Bill Clinton's presidential inauguration). She was also awarded more than fifty honorary degrees during her lifetime.

Angelou's was one of those rare voices of a generation that managed to elicit tangible and positive change, overcoming the challenges of racism and inequality with her unique talent for writing and expressing her ideas.

This book brings together some of Angelou's most interesting and inspiring thoughts on a variety of topics.

ABOUT HERSELF AND HER FAMILY

"I know that I'm not the easiest person to live with. The challenge I put on myself is so great that the person I live with feels himself challenged. I bring a lot to bear, and I don't know how not to."

*

"I don't know how much longer I'll be around. I'll probably be writing when the Lord says, 'Maya, Maya Angelou, it's time.'"

*

"I liked to write from the time I was about 12 or 13. I loved to read. And since I only spoke to my brother, I would write down my thoughts. And I think I wrote some of the worst poetry west of the Rockies. But by the time I was in my 20s, I found myself writing little essays and more poetry - writing at writing."

*

"I find in my poetry and prose the rhythms and imagery of the best - I mean, when I'm at my best - of the good Southern black preachers. The lyricism of the spirituals and the directness of gospel songs and the mystery of blues are in my music or in my poetry and prose, or I missed everything."

*

"Whenever something went wrong when I was young - if I had a pimple or if my hair broke - my mom would say, 'Sister mine, I'm going to make you some soup.' And I really thought the soup would make my pimple go away or my hair stronger."

*

"I'm very, very serious - I'm serious enough not to take myself too seriously. That means I can be completely wedded to the moment. But when I leave that moment, I want to be completely wedded to the next moment."

*

"My life has been one great big joke, a dance that's walked a song that's spoke, I laugh so hard I almost choke when I think about myself."

*

"I like to speak on matters which matter to human beings, and almost everything matters to human beings."

*

"One of my lungs is half gone, and the other half, because I smoked for years, has a lesion. So I can't swim anymore and had the swimming pool covered over. Now it's what I call the dance pavilion, and so

I and my friends sit out and put music on and watch people dance."

*

"On Saturday afternoons when all the things are done in the house and there's no real work to be done, I play Bach and Chopin and turn it up real loudly and get a good bottle of chardonnay and sit out on my deck and look out at the garden."

*

"I speak to the black experience, but I am always talking about the human condition."

*

"I've read everything Thomas Wolfe ever wrote; my brother and I memorized whole chapters of 'You Can't Go Home Again' and 'Look Homeward, Angel.'"

*

"I promised myself that I would write as well as I can, tell the truth, not to tell everything I know, but to make sure that everything I tell is true, as I understand it. And to use the eloquence which my language affords me."

*

"My life has been long, and believing that life loves the liver of it, I have dared to try many things, sometimes trembling, but daring still."

*

"I've always written. There's a journal which I kept from about 9 years old. The man who gave it to me lived across the street from the store and kept it when my grandmother's papers were destroyed. I'd written some essays. I loved poetry, still do. But I really, really loved it then."

*

"I'm not a writer who teaches. I'm a teacher who writes."

*

"I'm just someone who likes cooking and for whom sharing food is a form of expression."

*

"My greatest blessing has been the birth of my son. My next greatest blessing has been my ability to turn people into children of mine."

*

"Every December, I host a tree-trimming party. I serve chili with cornbread and lots of good wine. It's a wonderful party, and it shows how much adults like to play."

*

"I work very hard, and I play very hard. I'm grateful for life. And I live it - I believe life loves the liver of it. I live it."

*

"Some critics will write 'Maya Angelou is a natural writer' - which is right after being a natural heart surgeon."

*

"Black people comprehend the South. We understand its weight. It has rested on our backs... I knew that my heart would break if ever I put my foot down on that soil, moist, still, with old hurts. I had to face the fear/loathing at its source or it would consume me whole."

*

"I always knew from that moment, from the time I found myself at home in that little segregated library in the South, all the way up until I walked up the steps of the New York City library, I always felt, in any town, if I can get to a library, I'll be OK. It really helped me as a child, and that never left me."

*

"I keep a hotel room in my town, although I have a large house. And I go there at about 5:30 in the morning, and I start working. And I don't allow anybody to come in that room. I work on yellow pads and with ballpoint pens. I keep a Bible, a thesaurus, a dictionary, and a bottle of sherry. I stay there until midday."

*

"I was very blessed to have family and friends, but particularly family, who told me I was not only all right, I was just right, so I believe that my brain is a good one, and it's lasting me very well."

*

"I wasn't a pretty girl. I was six feet tall at 15, you know."

*

"I have a son, who is my heart. A wonderful young man, daring and loving and strong and kind."

*

"I wrote some of the worst poetry west from the Mississippi River, but I wrote. And I finally sometimes got it right."

*

"I do like to have guns around. I don't like to carry them. But I like - if somebody is going to come into my house and I have not put out the welcome mat, I want to stop them."

*

"Of course, there are those critics - New York critics as a rule - who say, 'Well, Maya Angelou has a new book out and of course it's good but then she's a natural writer.' Those are the ones I want to grab by the throat and wrestle to the floor because it takes me forever to get it to sing. I work at the language."

*

"When I write, I tend to twist my hair. Something for my small mind to do, I guess."

*

"I never expected anyone to take care of me, but in my wildest dreams and juvenile yearnings, I wanted the house with the picket fence from June Allyson movies. I knew that was yearning like one yearns to fly."

*

"My great hope is to laugh as much as I cry; to get my work done and try to love somebody and have the courage to accept the love in return."

*

"When younger writers and poets, musicians and painters are weakened by a stemming of funds, they come to me saddened, not as full of dreams and excitement and ideas. I am then weakened and diminished, and made less rich."

*

"My mother said I must always be intolerant of ignorance but understanding of illiteracy. That some people, unable to go to school, were more educated and more intelligent than college professors."

*

"I have a feeling that I make a very good friend, and I'm a good mother, and a good sister, and a good citizen. I am involved in life itself - all of it. And I have a lot of energy and a lot of nerve."

*

"If you were the President of the United States or the Queen of England - you couldn't have a person who would be more protective than my mother was for me. Which meant really that I could dare to do all sorts of things."

*

"I will not sit in a room with black people when the N word is used. I know it was meant to belittle a person, so I will not sit there and have that poison put on me. Now a black person can say, 'Oh, you know, I can use this word because I'm black.'"

*

"Like a pianist runs her fingers over the keys, I'll search my mind for what to say. Now, the poem may want you to write it. And then sometimes you see a situation and think, 'I'd like to write about that.' Those are two different ways of being approached by a poem, or approaching a poem."

*

"At fifteen life had taught me undeniably that surrender, in its place, was as honorable as resistance, especially if one had no choice."

*

"Music was my refuge. I could crawl into the space between the notes and curl my back to loneliness."

*

"I long, as does every human being, to be at home wherever I find myself."

*

"I know some people might think it odd - unworthy even - for me to have written a cookbook, but I make no apologies. The U.S. poet laureate Billy Collins thought I had demeaned myself by writing poetry for Hallmark Cards, but I am the people's poet so I write for the people."

*

"If I walked into the kitchen without washing my hands as a kid, I'd hear a loud 'A-hem!' from my mother or grandmother. Now I count on other people to do the same."

*

"Early on, I was so impressed with Charles Dickens. I grew up in the South, in a little village in Arkansas, and the whites in my town were really mean, and rude. Dickens, I could tell, wouldn't be a man who would curse me out and talk to me rudely."

*

"When I cook for my family on Christmas, I make feijoada, a South American dish of roasted and smoked meats like ham, pork, beef, lamb, and bacon - all served with black beans and rice. It's festive but different."

*

"My mission in life is not merely to survive, but to thrive; and to do so with some passion, some compassion, some humor, and some style."

*

"I am never proud to participate in violence, yet I know that each of us must care enough for ourselves that we can be ready and able to come to our own defence when and wherever needed."

*

"I write some country music. There's a song called 'I Hope You Dance.' Incredible. I was going to write that poem; somebody beat me to it."

*

"At one time in my life, from the time I was seven until I was about 13, I didn't speak. I only spoke to my brother. The reason I didn't speak: I had been molested, and I told the name of the molester to my brother who told it to the family."

*

"I've still not written as well as I want to. I want to write so that the reader in Des Moines, Iowa, in Kowloon, China, in Cape Town, South Africa, can say, 'You know, that's the truth. I wasn't there, and I wasn't a six-foot black girl, but that's the truth.'"

*

"I think I have had so much blessing - I've had my brother, who was brilliant - I think my family came closest to making a genius when they made my brother - Bailey was just all of that. He loved me."

*

"To take a few nouns, and a few pronouns, and adverbs and adjectives, and put them together, ball them up, and throw them against the wall to make them bounce. That's what Norman Mailer did. That's what James Baldwin did, and Joan Didion did, and that's what I do - that's what I mean to do."

*

"The need for change bulldozed a road down the center of my mind."

*

"I love a Hebrew National hot dog with an ice-cold Corona - no lime. If the phone rings, I won't answer until I'm done."

*

"I'm considered wise, and sometimes I see myself as knowing. Most of the time, I see myself as wanting to know. And I see myself as a very interested person. I've never been bored in my life."

*

"I am grateful to be a woman. I must have done something great in another life."

*

"At 50, I began to know who I was. It was like waking up to myself."

*

"I speak a number of languages, but none are more beautiful to me than English."

*

"I would be a liar, a hypocrite, or a fool - and I'm not any of those - to say that I don't write for the reader. I do. But for the reader who hears, who really will work at it, going behind what I seem to say. So I write for myself and that reader who will pay the dues."

*

"I respect myself and insist upon it from everybody. And because I do it, I then respect everybody, too."

*

"I learned a long time ago the wisest thing I can do is be on my own side, be an advocate for myself and others like me."

*

"I was a dancer for many years. I was a premier dancer with 'Porgy and Bess,' the opera. And I taught dance some, in different places."

*

"Cooking certain dishes, like roast pork, reminds me of my mother."

*

"Growing up, my grandmother did not want worldly

music in the house. Then when I went out to California, I started listening to Spanish music, mostly Mexican music. But were I in Egypt, I would listen to the music of the people, or if I was in Italy, I'd listen to Italian music."

*

"In so many ways, segregation shaped me, and education liberated me."

*

"It's so tedious writing cookbooks or writing the recipes because I've never been much of a measurer. But to write a book, you have to measure everything."

ABOUT LOVE

"I know for sure that loves saves me and that it is here to save us all."

*

"I could fall in love with a sumo wrestler if he told stories and made me laugh. Obviously, it would be easier if someone was African-American and lived next door and went to the same church. Because then I wouldn't have to translate."

*

"The loss of young first love is so painful that it

borders on the ludicrous."

*

"Love is like a virus. It can happen to anybody at any time."

*

"Love recognizes no barriers. It jumps hurdles, leaps fences, penetrates walls to arrive at its destination full of hope."

*

"Loving someone liberates the lover as well as the beloved. And that kind of love comes with age."

*

"You can't forgive without loving. And I don't mean sentimentality. I don't mean mush. I mean having enough courage to stand up and say, 'I forgive. I'm finished with it.'"

*

"The love of the family, the love of one person can heal. It heals the scars left by a larger society. A massive, powerful society."

*

"If we lose love and self respect for each other, this is how we finally die."

EQUALITY

"Until blacks and whites see each other as brother and sister, we will not have parity. It's very clear."

*

"Information helps you to see that you're not alone. That there's somebody in Mississippi and somebody in Tokyo who all have wept, who've all longed and lost, who've all been happy. So the library helps you to see, not only that you are not alone, but that you're not really any different from everyone else."

*

"It is impossible to struggle for civil rights, equal rights for blacks, without including whites. Because equal rights, fair play, justice, are all like the air: we all have it, or none of us has it. That is the truth of it."

*

"It's good to remember that in crises, natural crises, human beings forget for awhile their ignorances, their biases, their prejudices. For a little while, neighbors help neighbors and strangers help strangers."

*

"We can learn to see each other and see ourselves in each other and recognize that human beings are more alike than we are unalike."

*

"As far as I knew white women were never lonely, except in books. White men adored them, Black men desired them and Black women worked for them."

*

"A black person grows up in this country - and in many places - knowing that racism will be as familiar as salt to the tongue. Also, it can be as dangerous as too much salt. I think that you must struggle for betterment for yourself and for everyone."

*

"All great artists draw from the same resource: the human heart, which tells us that we are all more alike than we are unalike."

*

"Most plain girls are virtuous because of the scarcity of opportunity to be otherwise."

*

"At one time, you could sit on the Rue de la Paix in Paris or at the Habima Theater in Tel Aviv or in Medina and you could see a person come in, black, white, it didn't matter. You said, 'That's an American' because there's a readiness to smile and to talk to people."

*

"The poetry you read has been written for you, each of you - black, white, Hispanic, man, woman, gay, straight."

*

"I refuse to allow any man-made differences to separate me from any other human beings."

*

"When the human race neglects its weaker members, when the family neglects its weakest one - it's the first blow in a suicidal movement. I see the neglect in cities around the country, in poor white children in West Virginia and Virginia and Kentucky - in the big cities, too, for that matter."

*

"Growing up, I decided, a long time ago, I wouldn't accept any manmade differences between human beings, differences made at somebody else's insistence or someone else's whim or convenience."

*

"I never had that feeling that I had to carry the weight of somebody's ignorance around with me. And that was true for racists who wanted to use the 'n' word when talking about me or about my people, or the stupidity of people who really wanted to belittle other folks because they weren't pretty or they weren't rich or they weren't clever."

GENERAL THOUGHTS & OPINIONS

"I don't think there's such a thing as autobiographical fiction. If I say it happened, it happened, even if only in my mind."

*

"The idea is to write it so that people hear it and it slides through the brain and goes straight to the heart."

*

"A cynical young person is almost the saddest sight to see, because it means that he or she has gone from knowing nothing to believing nothing."

*

"The fact that the adult American Negro female emerges a formidable character is often met with amazement, distaste and even belligerance. It is seldom accepted as an inevitable outcome of the struggle won by survivors, and deserves respect if not enthusiastic acceptance."

*

"One of the wonderful things about Oprah: She teaches you to keep on stepping."

*

"Bitterness is cancer - it eats upon the host. It doesn't do anything to the object of its displeasure."

*

"Words mean more than what is set down on paper. It takes the human voice to infuse them with deeper meaning."

*

"I like chicken a lot because chicken is generous - that is to say, it's obedient. It will do whatever you tell it to do."

*

"I love to see a young girl go out and grab the world by the lapels."

*

"If one is lucky, a solitary fantasy can totally transform one million realities."

*

"How important it is for us to recognize and celebrate our heroes and she-roes!"

*

"Eating is so intimate. It's very sensual. When you invite someone to sit at your table and you want to cook for them, you're inviting a person into your life."

*

"The best comfort food will always be greens, cornbread, and fried chicken."

*

"In a magazine, one can get - from cover to cover - 15 to 20 different ideas about life and how to live it."

*

"During bad circumstances, which is the human inheritance, you must decide not to be reduced. You have your humanity, and you must not allow anything to reduce that. We are obliged to know we are global citizens. Disasters remind us we are world citizens, whether we like it or not."

*

"The hope, the hope that lives in the breast of the black American, is just so tremendous that it overwhelms me sometimes."

*

"Any book that helps a child to form a habit of reading, to make reading one of his deep and continuing needs, is good for him."

*

"It is a no-fail, incontrovertible reality: If you get, give. If you learn, teach. You can't do anything with that except do it."

*

"Children's talent to endure stems from their ignorance of alternatives."

*

"While the rest of the world has been improving technology, Ghana has been improving the quality of man's humanity to man."

*

"Elimination of illiteracy is as serious an issue to our history as the abolition of slavery."

*

"It is time for parents to teach young people early on that in diversity there is beauty and there is strength."

*

"When a person is going through hell, and she encounters someone who went through hellish hell and survived, then she can say, 'Mine is not so bad as all that. She came through, and so can I.'"

*

"The most important thing I can tell you about aging is this: If you really feel that you want to have an off-the-shoulder blouse and some big beads and thong sandals and a dirndl skirt and a magnolia in your hair, do it. Even if you're wrinkled."

*

"I think Clinton, after getting into office and into Washington, was shocked at being bludgeoned. So he spent time trying to be all things to all people - one way guaranteed not to be successful or respected in a lion's den. You can't just play around with all those big cats - you've got to take somebody on."

*

"Independence is a heady draught, and if you drink it in your youth, it can have the same effect on the brain as young wine does. It does not matter that its taste is not always appealing. It is addictive and with each drink you want more."

*

"I think music is one of the hero/sheroes of the African-American existence."

*

"I think a number of the leaders are, whether you like it or not, in the hip-hop generation. And when they understand enough, they'll do wonders. I count on them."

*

"How wonderful it is to be an American. We have known the best of times and the worst of times."

*

"Easy reading is damn hard writing. But if it's right, it's easy. It's the other way round, too. If it's slovenly written, then it's hard to read. It doesn't give the reader what the careful writer can give the reader."

*

"Writing and cookery are just two different means of communication."

*

"Effective action is always unjust."

GOD & RELIGION

"I'm a religious woman. And I feel I have responsibility. I have no modesty at all. I'm even afraid of it - it's a learned affectation and it's just stuck on me like decals. Now I pray for humility because that comes from inside out."

*

"I know that when I pray, something wonderful happens. Not just to the person or persons for whom I'm praying, but also something wonderful happens to me. I'm grateful that I'm heard."

*

"I thank God I'm myself and for the life I'm given to live and for friends and lovers and beloveds, and I thank God for knowing that all those people have already paid for me."

*

"In a long meter hymn, a singer - they call it 'lays out a line.' And then the whole church joins in in repeating that line. And they form a wall of harmony so tight, you can't wedge a pin between it."

*

"Whenever I want to laugh, I read a wonderful book, 'Children's Letters to God.' You can open it anywhere. One I read recently said, 'Dear God, thank you for the baby brother, but what I prayed for was a puppy.'"

*

"I'm working at trying to be a Christian, and that's serious business. It's like trying to be a good Jew, a good Muslim, a good Buddhist, a good Shintoist, a good Zoroastrian, a good friend, a good lover, a good mother, a good buddy - it's serious business."

*

"I'm just like you - I want to be a good human being. I'm doing my best, and I'm working at it. And I'm trying to be a Christian. I'm always amazed when people walk up to me and say, 'I'm a Christian.' I always think, 'Already? You've already got it?' I'm working at it. And at my age, I'll still be working at it at 96."

*

"Fighting for one's freedom, struggling towards being free, is like struggling to be a poet or a good Christian or a good Jew or a good Muslim or good Zen Buddhist. You work all day long and achieve some kind of level of success by nightfall, go to sleep and wake up the next morning with the job still to be done. So you start all over again."

*

"While I know myself as a creation of God, I am also obligated to realize and remember that everyone else and everything else are also God's creation."

*

"Everybody born comes from the Creator trailing wisps of glory. We come from the Creator with creativity. I think that each one of us is born with creativity."

*

"My grandmother took me to church on Sunday all day long, every Sunday into the night. Then Monday evening was the missionary meeting. Tuesday evening was usher board meeting. Wednesday evening was prayer meeting. Thursday evening was visit the sick. Friday evening was choir practice. I mean, and at all those gatherings, we sang."

*

"And if a person is religious, I think it's good, it helps you a bit. But if you're not, at least you can have the sense that there is a condition inside you which looks at the stars with amazement and awe."

HISTORY

"The more you know of your history, the more liberated you are."

*

"It's still scary every time I go back to the past. Each morning, my heart catches. When I get there, I remember how the light was, where the draft was coming from, what odors were in the air. When I write, I get all the weeping out."

*

"For Africa to me... is more than a glamorous fact.

It is a historical truth. No man can know where he is going unless he knows exactly where he has been and exactly how he arrived at his present place."

*

"History, despite its wrenching pain, cannot be unlived, but if faced with courage, need not be lived again."

*

"We are braver and wiser because they existed, those strong women and strong men... We are who we are because they were who they were. It's wise to know where you come from, who called your name."

*

"I long for the time when all human history is taught as one history, because it really is."

*

"I have great respect for the past. If you don't know where you've come from, you don't know where you're going. I have respect for the past, but I'm a person of the moment. I'm here, and I do my best to be completely centered at the place I'm at, then I go forward to the next place."

*

"Won't it be wonderful when black history and native American history and Jewish history and all of U.S. history is taught from one book. Just U.S. history."

*

"The first decade of the twentieth century was not a great time to be born black and poor and female in St. Louis, Missouri, but Vivian Baxter was born black and poor, to black and poor parents. Later she would grow up and be called beautiful. As a grown woman she would be known as the butter-colored lady with the blowback hair."

PEOPLE

"I think we all have empathy. We may not have enough courage to display it."

*

"I'm always disappointed when people don't live up to their potential. I know that a number of people look down on themselves and consequently on everybody who looks like them. But that, too, can change."

*

"I admire people who dare to take the language,

English, and understand it and understand the melody."

*

"I'm grateful to intelligent people. That doesn't mean educated. That doesn't mean intellectual. I mean really intelligent. What black old people used to call 'mother wit' means intelligence that you had in your mother's womb. That's what you rely on. You know what's right to do."

*

"I've learned that people will forget what you said, people will forget what you did, but people will never forget how you made them feel."

*

"Whenever I'm around some who is modest, I think, 'Run like hell and all of fire.' You don't want modesty, you want humility."

*

"It's very important to know the neighbor next door and the people down the street and the people in another race."

*

"Perhaps travel cannot prevent bigotry, but by demonstrating that all peoples cry, laugh, eat, worry, and die, it can introduce the idea that if we try and understand each other, we may even become friends."

*

"Modesty is a learned affectation. And as soon as life slams the modest person against the wall, that modesty drops."

*

"The ache for home lives in all of us, the safe place where we can go as we are and not be questioned."

*

"If we accept being talked to any kind of a way, then we are telling ourselves we are not quite worth the best. And if we have the effrontery to talk to anybody with less than courtesy, we tell ourselves and the world we are not very intelligent."

*

"Human beings love poetry. They don't even know it sometimes... whether they're the songs of Bono, or the songs of Justin Bieber... they're listening to poetry."

*

"All of us knows, not what is expedient, not what is going to make us popular, not what the policy is, or the company policy - but in truth each of us knows what is the right thing to do. And that's how I am guided."

*

"I believe that every person is born with talent."

*

"Somehow, we have come to the erroneous belief that we are all but flesh, blood, and bones, and that's all. So we direct our values to material things."

*

"If you're a human being, you can attempt to do what other human beings have done. We don't understand talent any more than we understand electricity."

*

"We allow our ignorance to prevail upon us and make us think we can survive alone, alone in patches, alone in groups, alone in races, even alone in genders."

*

"There's something which impels us to show our inner souls. The more courageous we are, the more we succeed in explaining what we know."

*

"Our stories come from our lives and from the playwright's pen, the mind of the actor, the roles we create, the artistry of life itself and the quest for peace."

PHILOSOPHY

"When someone shows you who they are, believe them the first time."

*

"What is a fear of living? It's being preeminently afraid of dying. It is not doing what you came here to do, out of timidity and spinelessness. The antidote is to take full responsibility for yourself - for the time you take up and the space you occupy. If you don't know what you're here to do, then just do some good."

*

"Bitterness is like cancer. It eats upon the host. But anger is like fire. It burns it all clean."

*

"We may encounter many defeats but we must not be defeated."

*

"I've learned that you shouldn't go through life with a catcher's mitt on both hands; you need to be able to throw something back."

*

"Nothing succeeds like success. Get a little success, and then just get a little more."

*

"Self-pity in its early stage is as snug as a feather mattress. Only when it hardens does it become uncomfortable."

*

"There is a very fine line between loving life and being greedy for it."

*

"Whatever you want to do, if you want to be great at it, you have to love it and be able to make sacrifices for it."

*

"If you find it in your heart to care for somebody else, you will have succeeded."

*

"Achievement brings its own anticlimax."

*

"I have found that among its other benefits, giving liberates the soul of the giver."

*

"You may not control all the events that happen to you, but you can decide not to be reduced by them."

*

"It's one of the greatest gifts you can give yourself, to forgive. Forgive everybody."

*

"Don't get older just to get wiser. If you get older, you will be wiser, I believe that - if you dare. But get older because it's fun!"

*

"Nothing will work unless you do."

*

"Don't let the incidents which take place in life bring you low. And certainly don't whine. You can be brought low, that's OK, but don't be reduced by them. Just say, 'That's life.'"

*

"If you don't like something, change it. If you can't change it, change your attitude. Don't complain."

*

"Hold those things that tell your history and protect them. During slavery, who was able to read or write or keep anything? The ability to have somebody to tell your story to is so important. It says: 'I was here. I may be sold tomorrow. But you know I was here.'"

*

"You have to develop ways so that you can take up for yourself, and then you take up for someone else. And so sooner or later, you have enough courage to really stand up for the human race and say, 'I'm a representative.'"

*

"All great achievements require time."

*

"Everyone has at least one story, and each of us is funny if we admit it. You have to admit you're the funniest person you've ever heard of."

*

"There's a world of difference between truth and facts. Facts can obscure the truth."

*

"Try to be a rainbow in someone's cloud."

*

"Life loves to be taken by the lapel and told: 'I'm

with you kid. Let's go.'"

*

"Once you appreciate one of your blessings, one of your senses, your sense of hearing, then you begin to respect the sense of seeing and touching and tasting, you learn to respect all the senses."

*

"Courage - you develop courage by doing small things like just as if you wouldn't want to pick up a 100-pound weight without preparing yourself."

THOUGHT PROVOKING WORDS OF WISDOM

"We have to confront ourselves. Do we like what we see in the mirror? And, according to our light, according to our understanding, according to our courage, we will have to say yea or nay - and rise!"

*

"Find a beautiful piece of art. If you fall in love with Van Gogh or Matisse or John Oliver Killens, or if you fall love with the music of Coltrane, the music of Aretha Franklin, or the music of Chopin - find some beautiful art and admire it, and realize that that was created by human beings just like you, no more human, no less."

*

"There is no greater agony than bearing an untold story inside you."

*

"A wise woman wishes to be no one's enemy; a wise woman refuses to be anyone's victim."

*

"Prejudice is a burden that confuses the past, threatens the future and renders the present inaccessible."

*

"If you want what you're saying heard, then take your time and say it so that the listener will actually hear it. You might save somebody's life. Your own, first."

*

"A bird doesn't sing because it has an answer, it sings because it has a song."

*

"The thing to do, it seems to me, is to prepare yourself so you can be a rainbow in somebody else's cloud. Somebody who may not look like you. May not call God the same name you call God - if they call God at all. I may not dance your dances or speak your language. But be a blessing to somebody. That's what I think."

*

"You are the sum total of everything you've ever seen, heard, eaten, smelled, been told, forgot - it's all there. Everything influences each of us, and because of that I try to make sure that my experiences are positive."

*

"If you have only one smile in you give it to the people you love."

*

"What humility does for one is it reminds us that there are people before me. I have already been paid for. And what I need to do is prepare myself so that I can pay for someone else who has yet to come but who may be here and needs me."

*

"If you're serious, you really understand that it's important that you laugh as much as possible and admit that you're the funniest person you ever met. You have to laugh. Admit that you're funny. Otherwise, you die in solemnity."

*

"I'm convinced of this: Good done anywhere is good done everywhere. For a change, start by speaking to people rather than walking by them like they're stones that don't matter. As long as you're breathing, it's never too late to do some good."

*

"The truth is, no one of us can be free until everybody is free."

*

"We write for the same reason that we walk, talk, climb mountains or swim the oceans - because we can. We have some impulse within us that makes us want to explain ourselves to other human beings. That's why we paint, that's why we dare to love someone - because we have the impulse to explain who we are."

*

"In all my work, I try to say - 'You may be given a load of sour lemons, why not try to make a dozen lemon meringue pies?'"

*

"That's the biggest gift I can give anybody: 'Wake up, be aware of who you are, what you're doing and what you can do to prevent yourself from becoming ill.'"

*

"Those of us who submitted or surrendered our ideas and dreams and identities to the 'leaders' must take back our rights, our identities, our responsibilities."

*

"One isn't necessarily born with courage, but one is born with potential. Without courage, we cannot practice any other virtue with consistency. We can't be kind, true, merciful, generous, or honest."

*

"I love wisdom. And you can never be great at anything unless you love it. Not be in love with it, but love the thing, admire the thing. And it seems that if you love the thing, and you don't just want to possess it, it will find you."

*

"Encouragement to all women is - let us try to offer help before we have to offer therapy. That is to say, let's see if we can't prevent being ill by trying to offer a love of prevention before illness."

*

"If we don't plant the right things, we will reap the wrong things. It goes without saying. And you don't have to be, you know, a brilliant biochemist and you don't have to have an IQ of 150. Just common sense tells you to be kind, ninny, fool. Be kind."

ALSO BY FRANK JOHNSON

INSIDE THE MIND OF CHUCK PALAHNIUK

THE WIT AND WISDOM OF JOSS WHEDON

INSIDE THE MIND OF EMMA WATSON

THE VERY BEST OF MICHAEL MOORE

THE PHILOSOPHY OF PAUL WATSON

INSIDE THE MIND OF STEPHEN HAWKING

Made in United States
North Haven, CT
24 February 2022

16436565R00046